ISBN- 13:978-1542909860

Printed in The United States of America

Welcome to an adventure with the Majestic Letter M

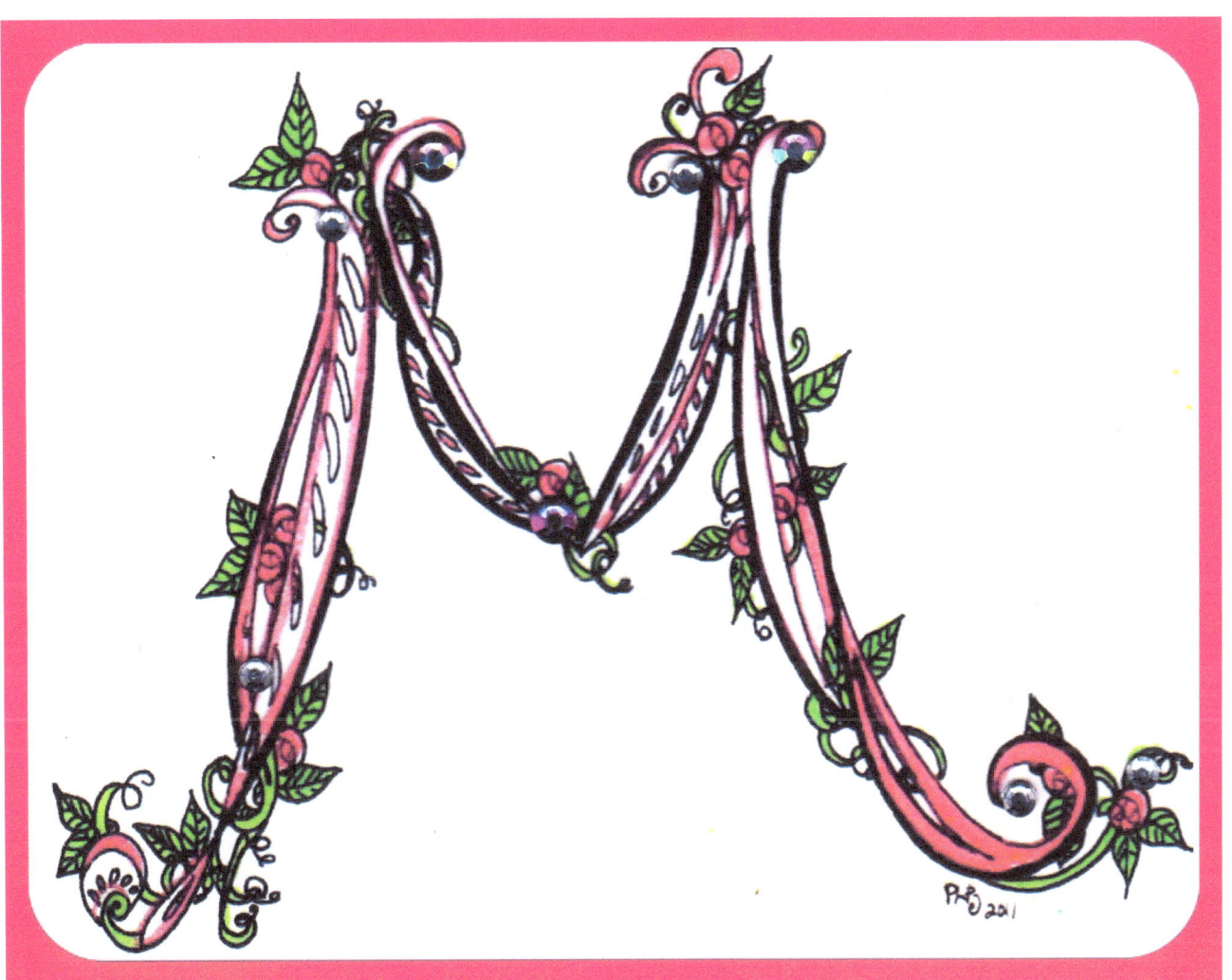

The Majestic Letter M
Coloring Book

By Peggy Louise Parrish
C. 2017

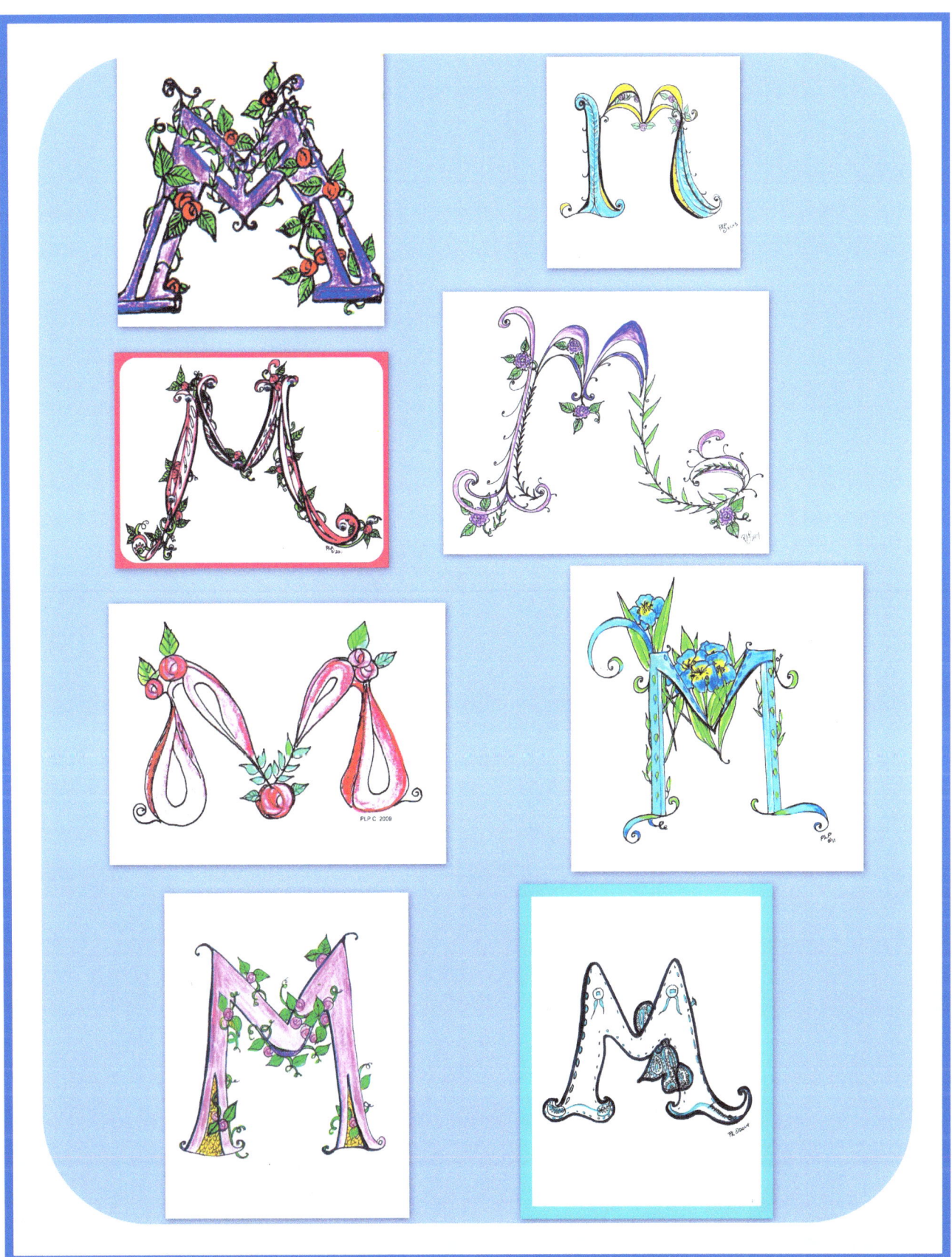

As you begin your Letter M coloring adventure think of all the wonderful names and words that begin with M. Maybe your own first or last name begins with M. You may make a few "in house" M letter copies if you want to try to color them several different ways. Experiment and enjoy. Make one into a card perhaps. I only ask that you don't sell anything you make with these letters. Leave the initials at the bottom of the designed letters. Quality colored pencils are the medium most often enjoyed with these letter pages. If you choose watercolor pencils, paints or markers be sure to place a scrap paper under your work.

Don't hesitate to write colored by...... and your own name on your colored work. May my letters bring you joy . PLP

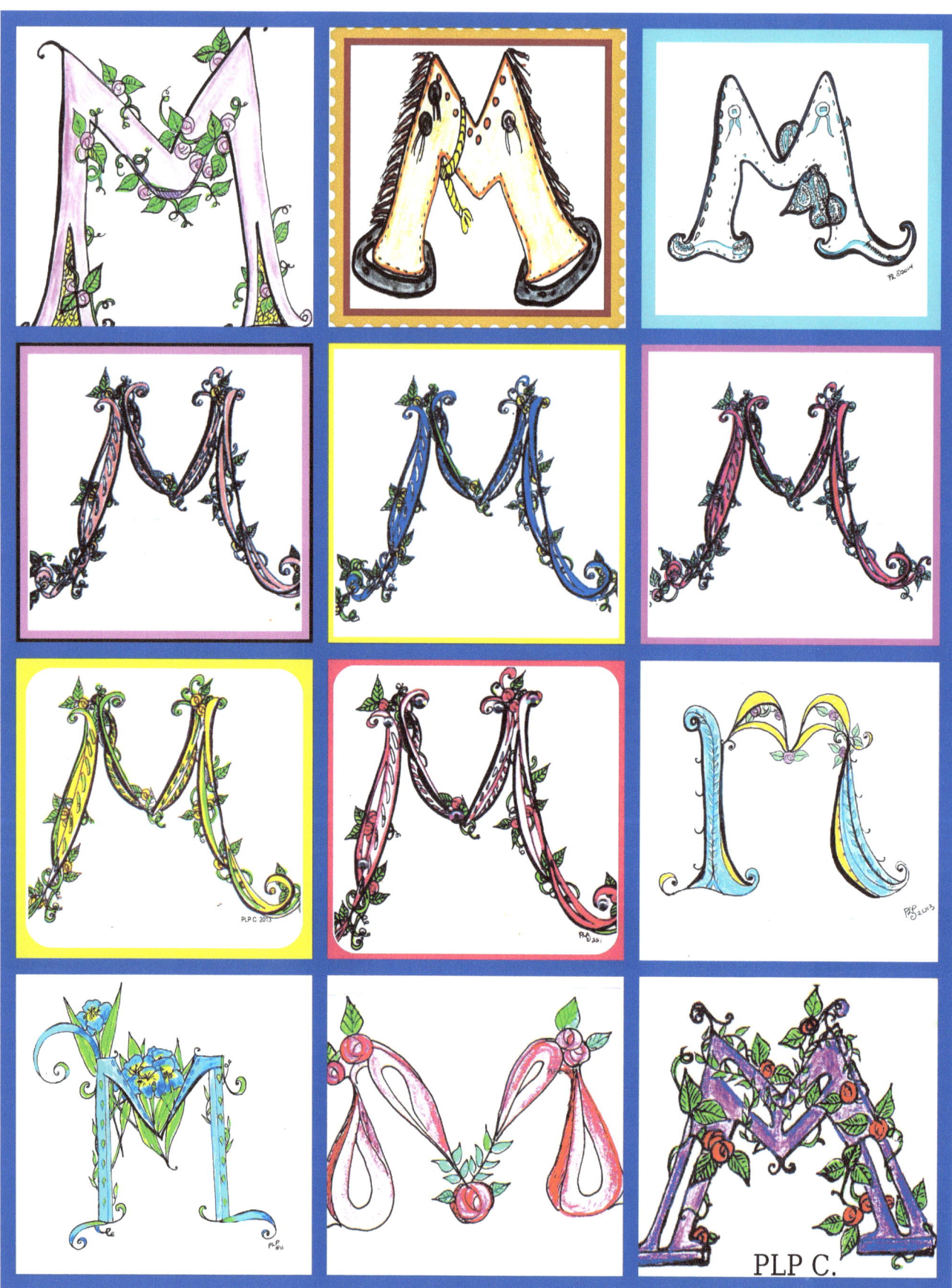

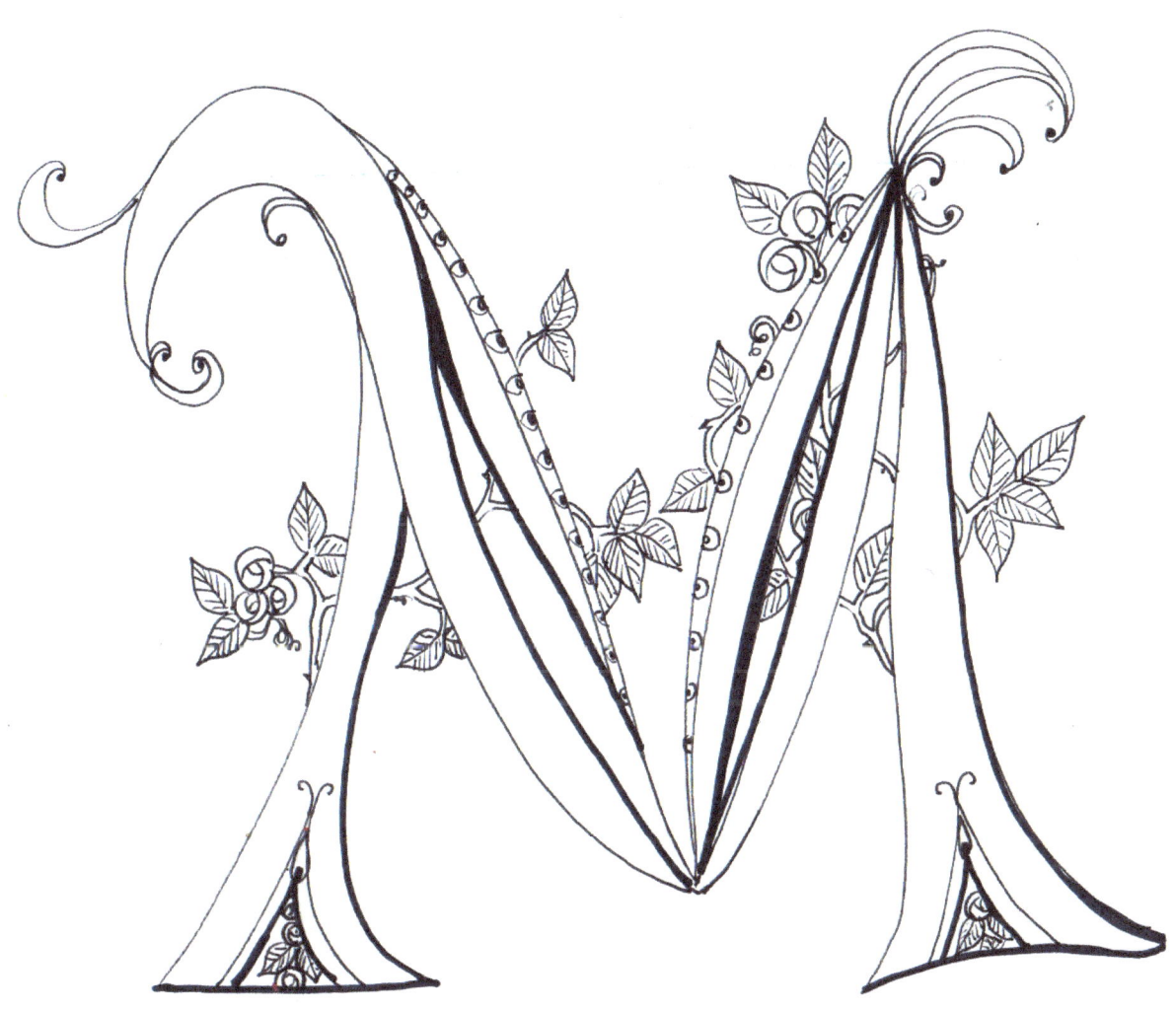

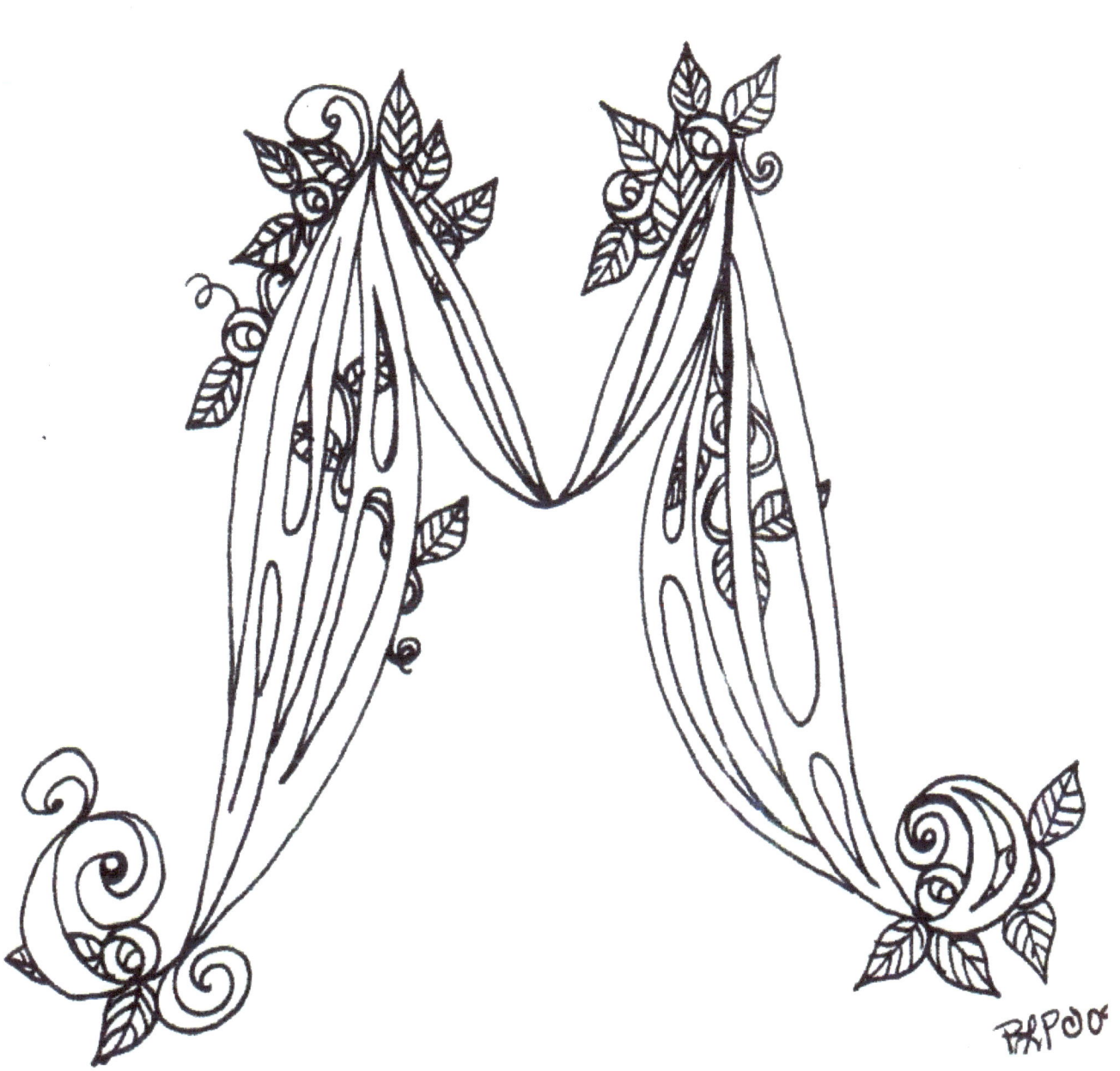

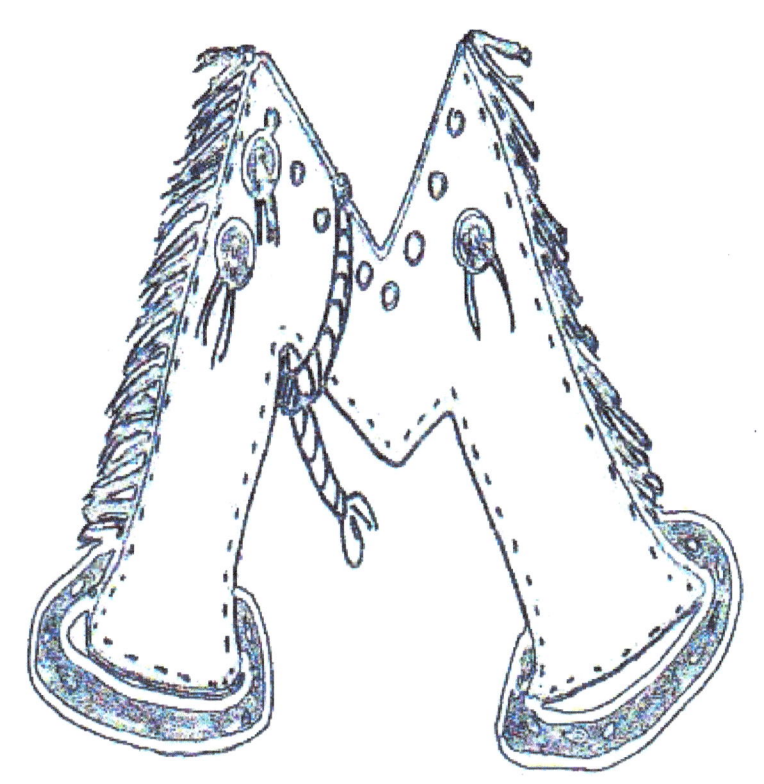

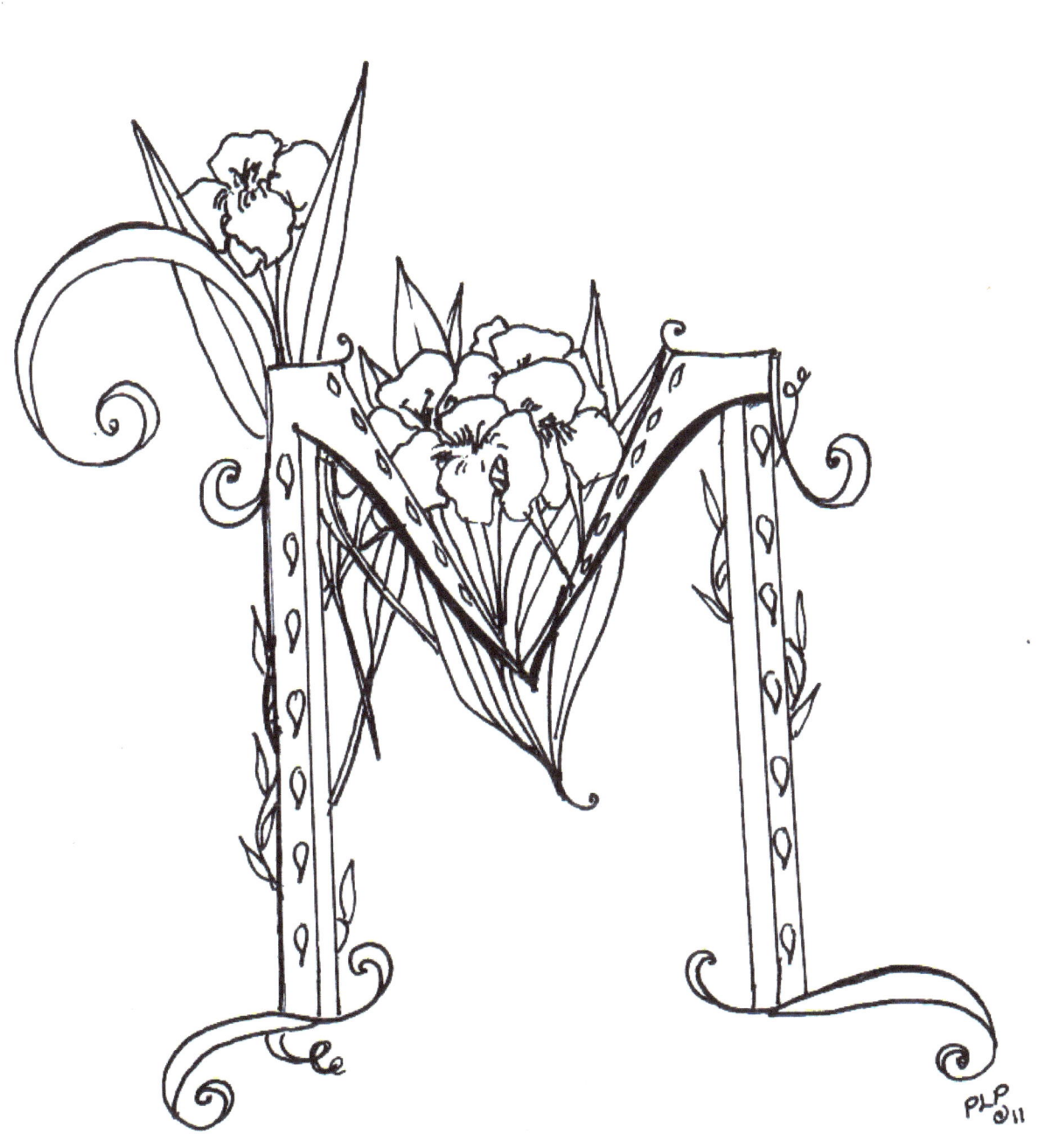

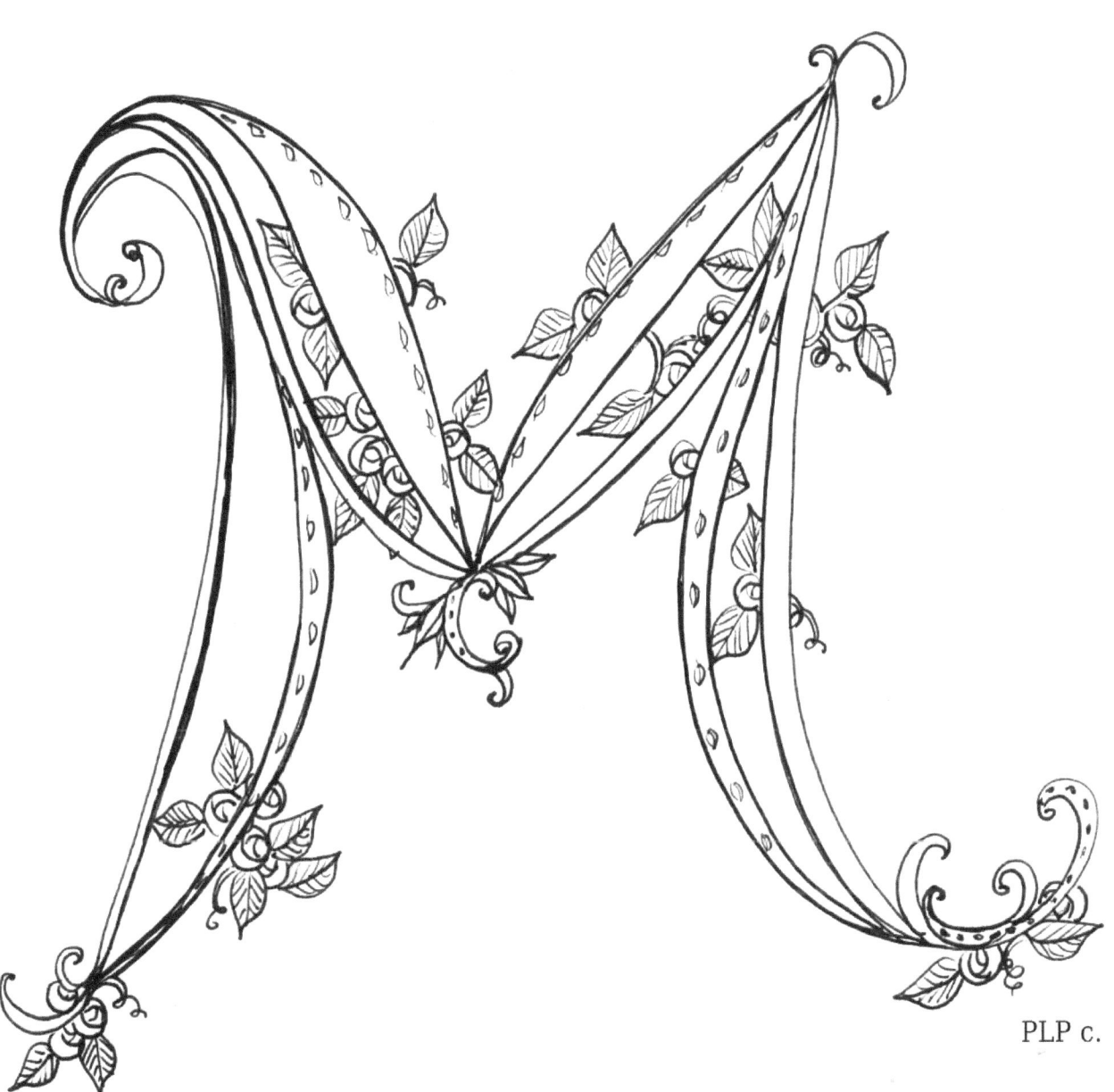

PLP c.

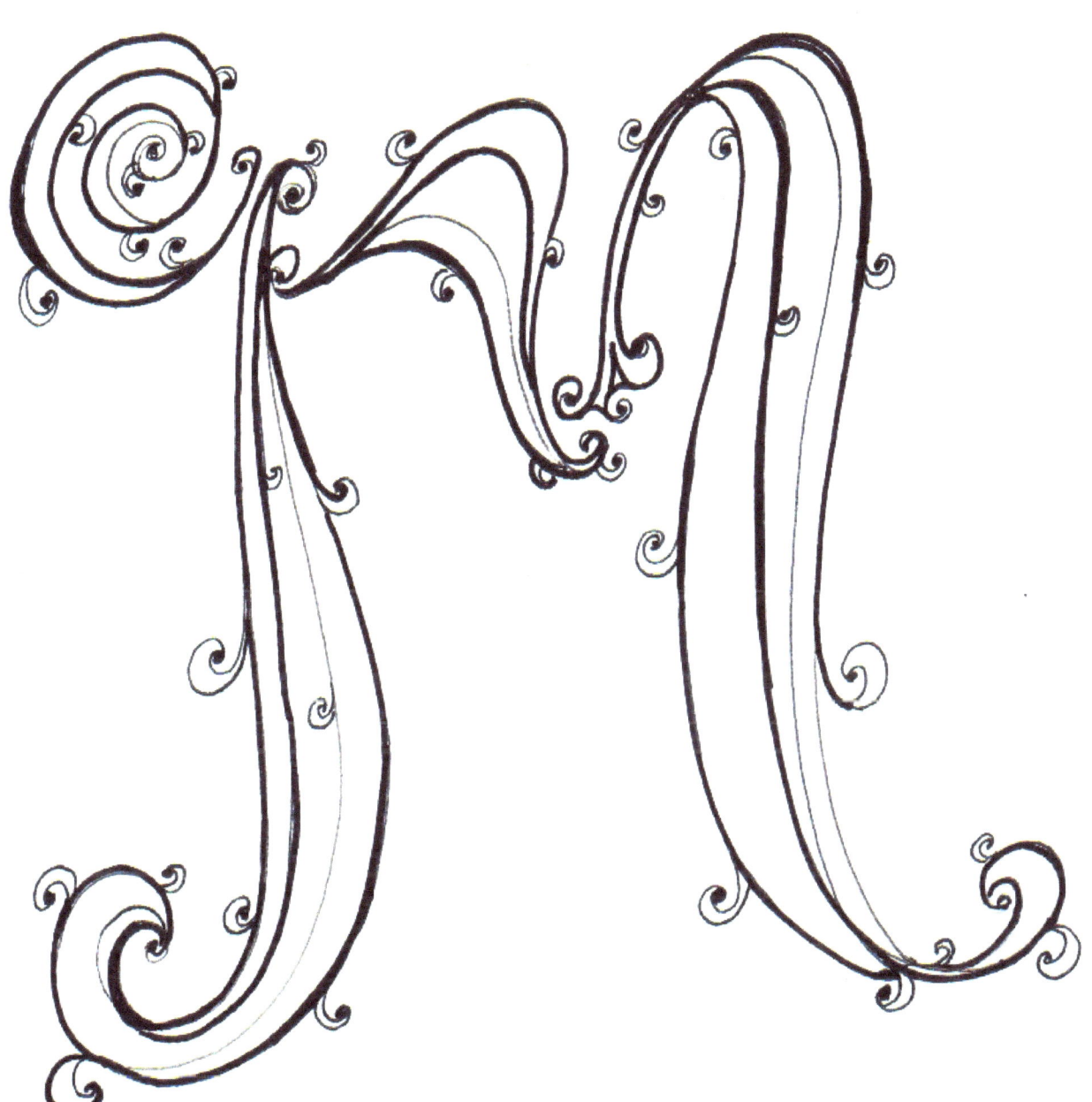

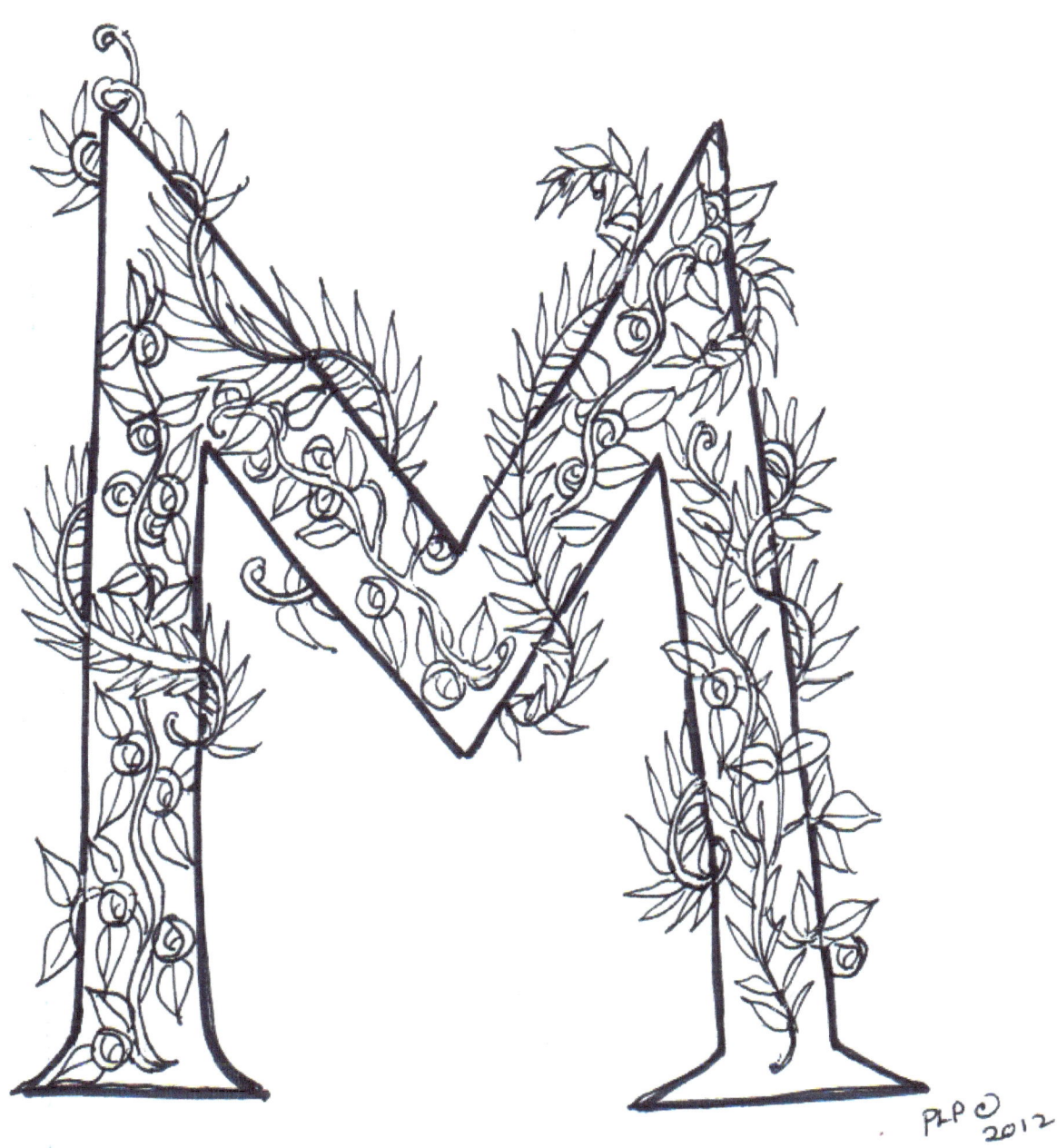

PLP © 2012

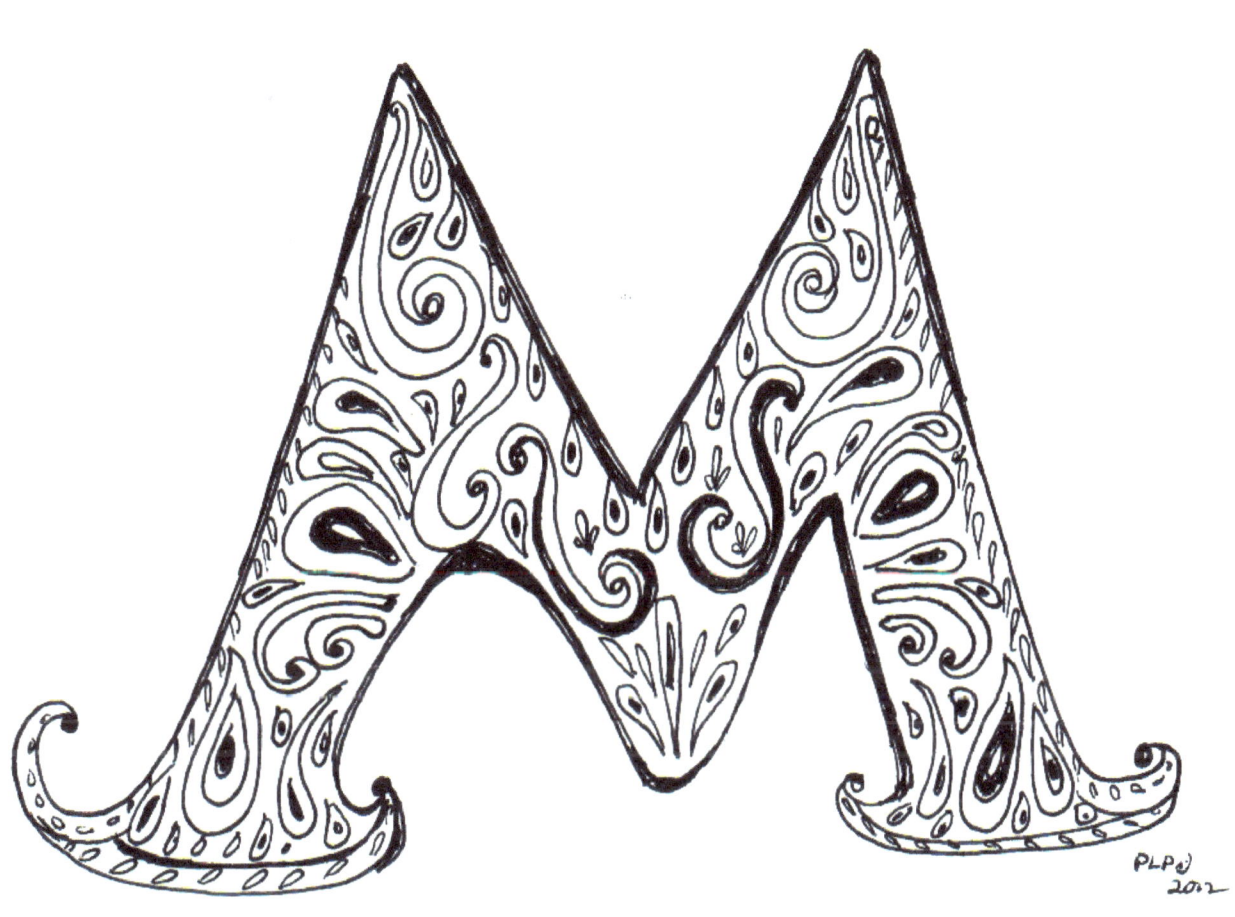

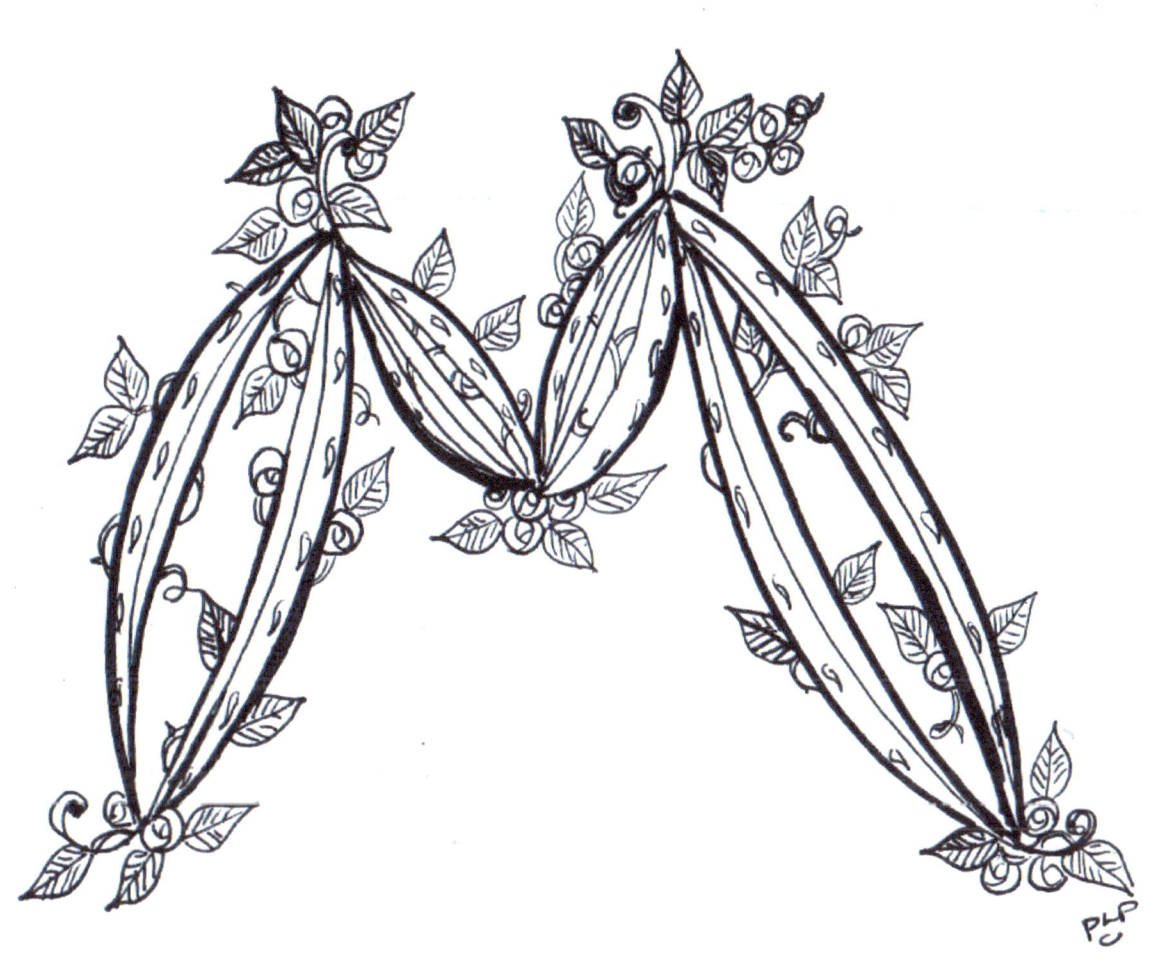

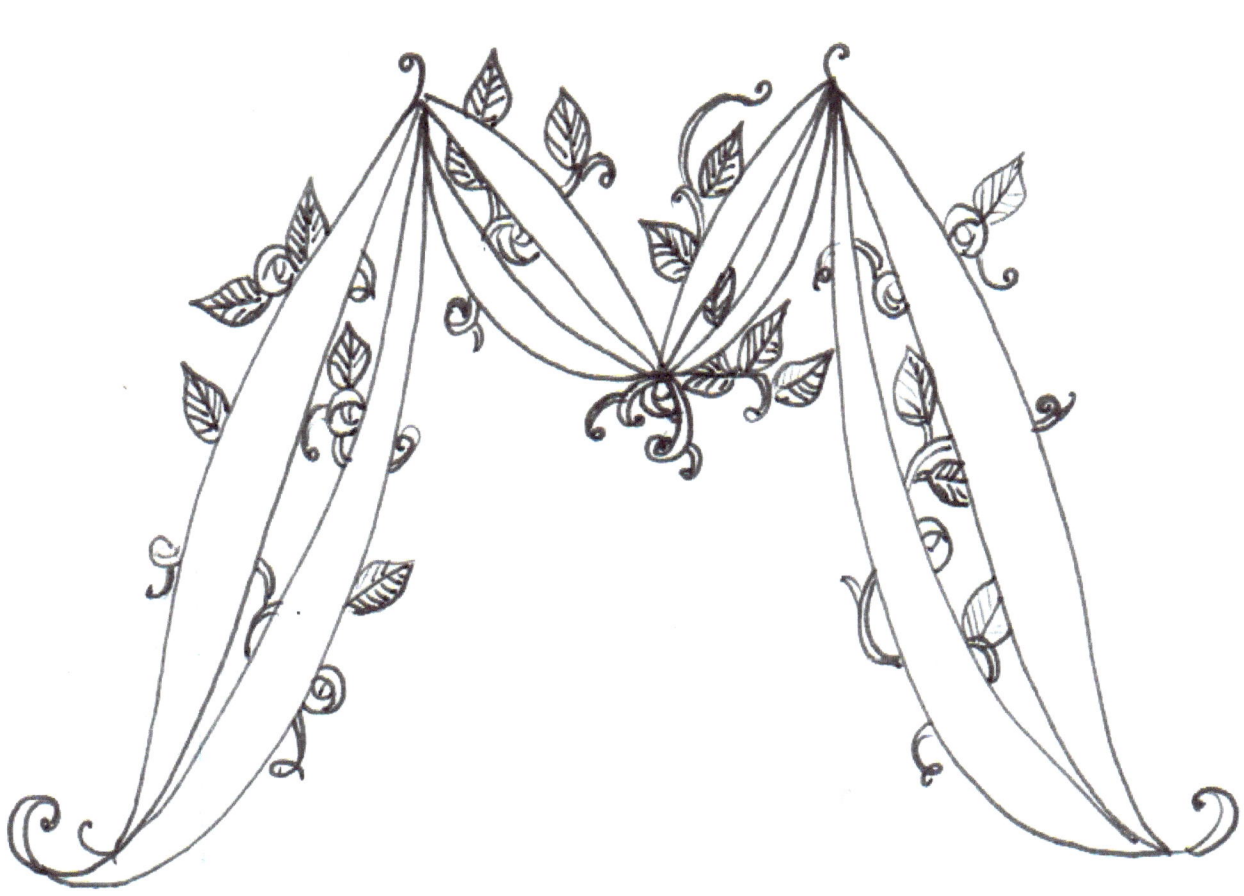

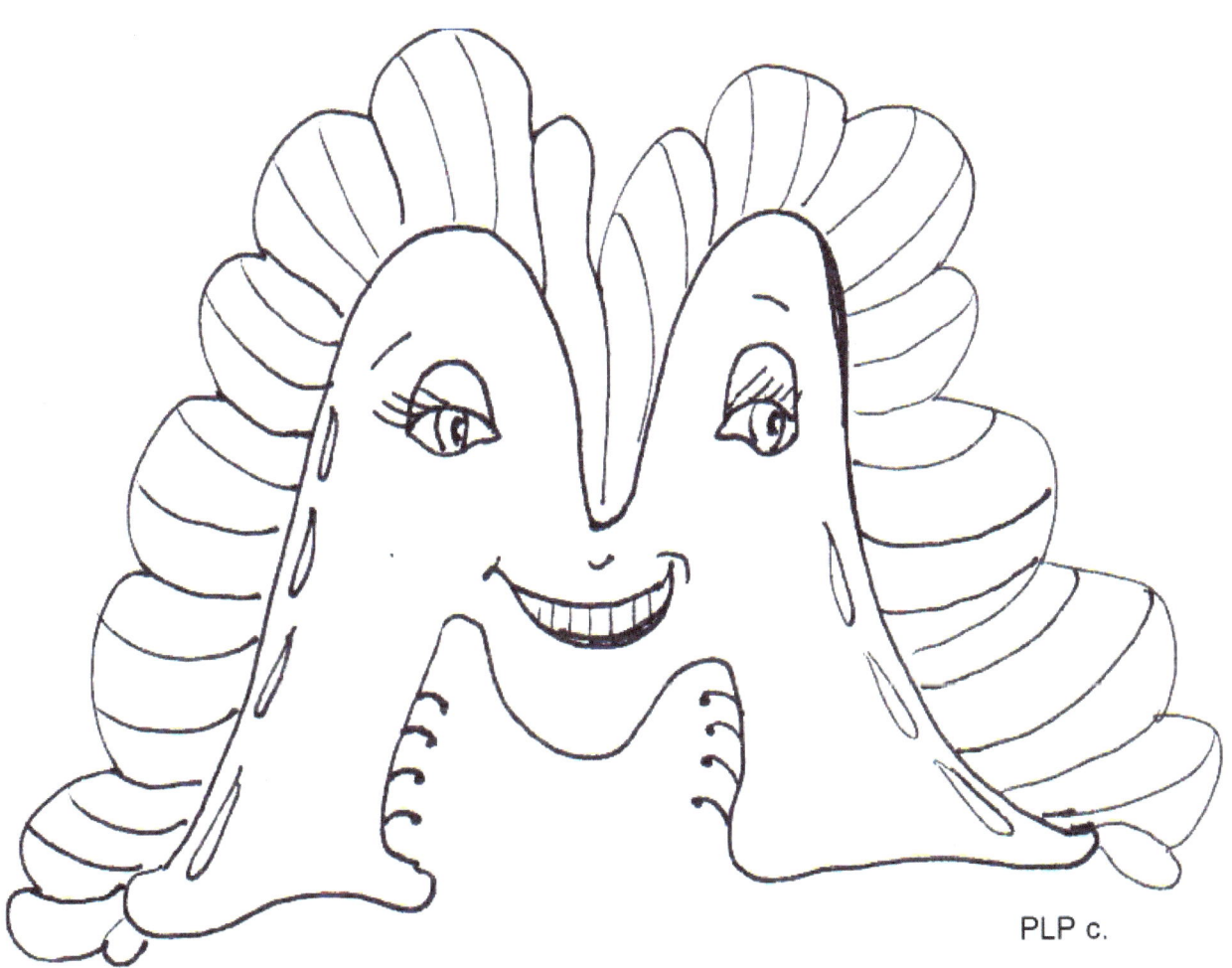

PLP c.

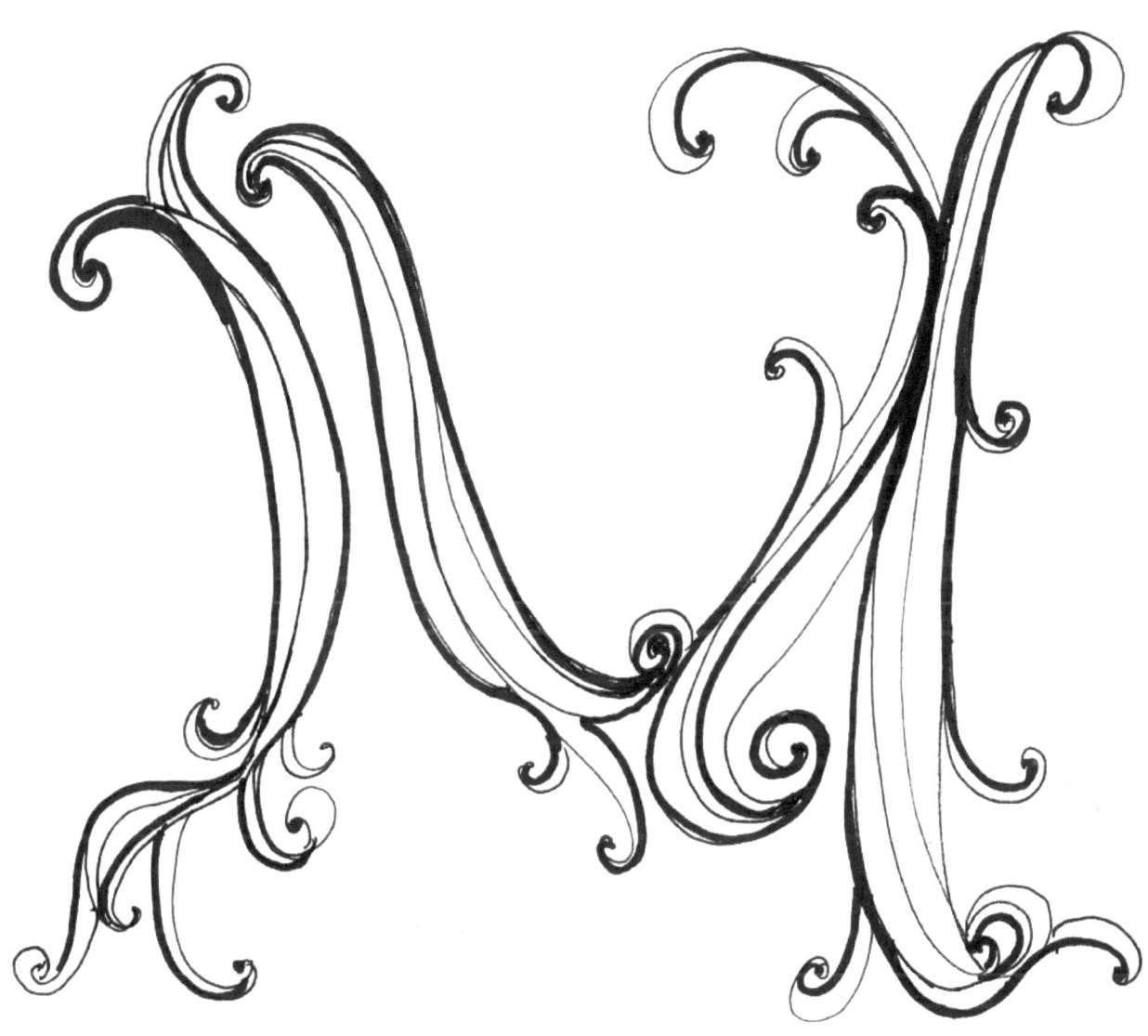

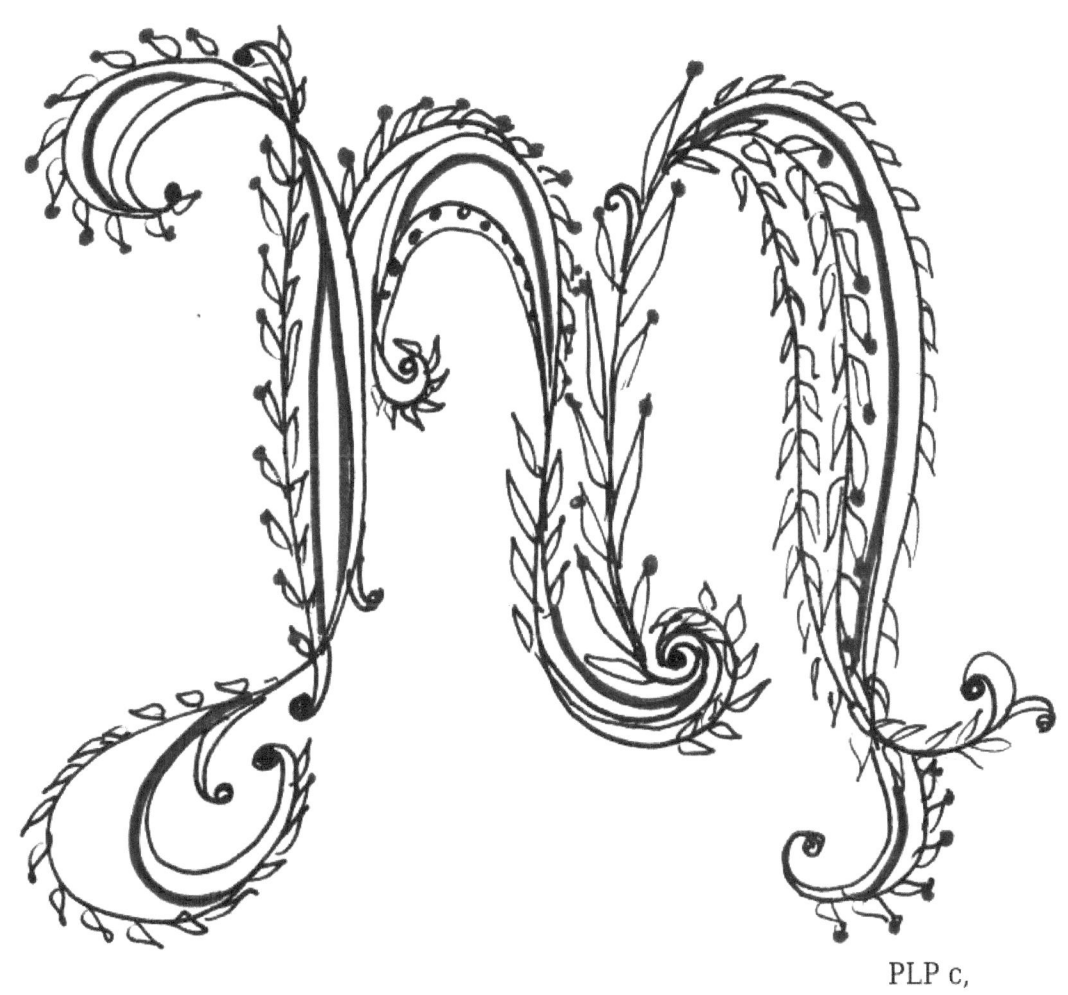

PLP c,

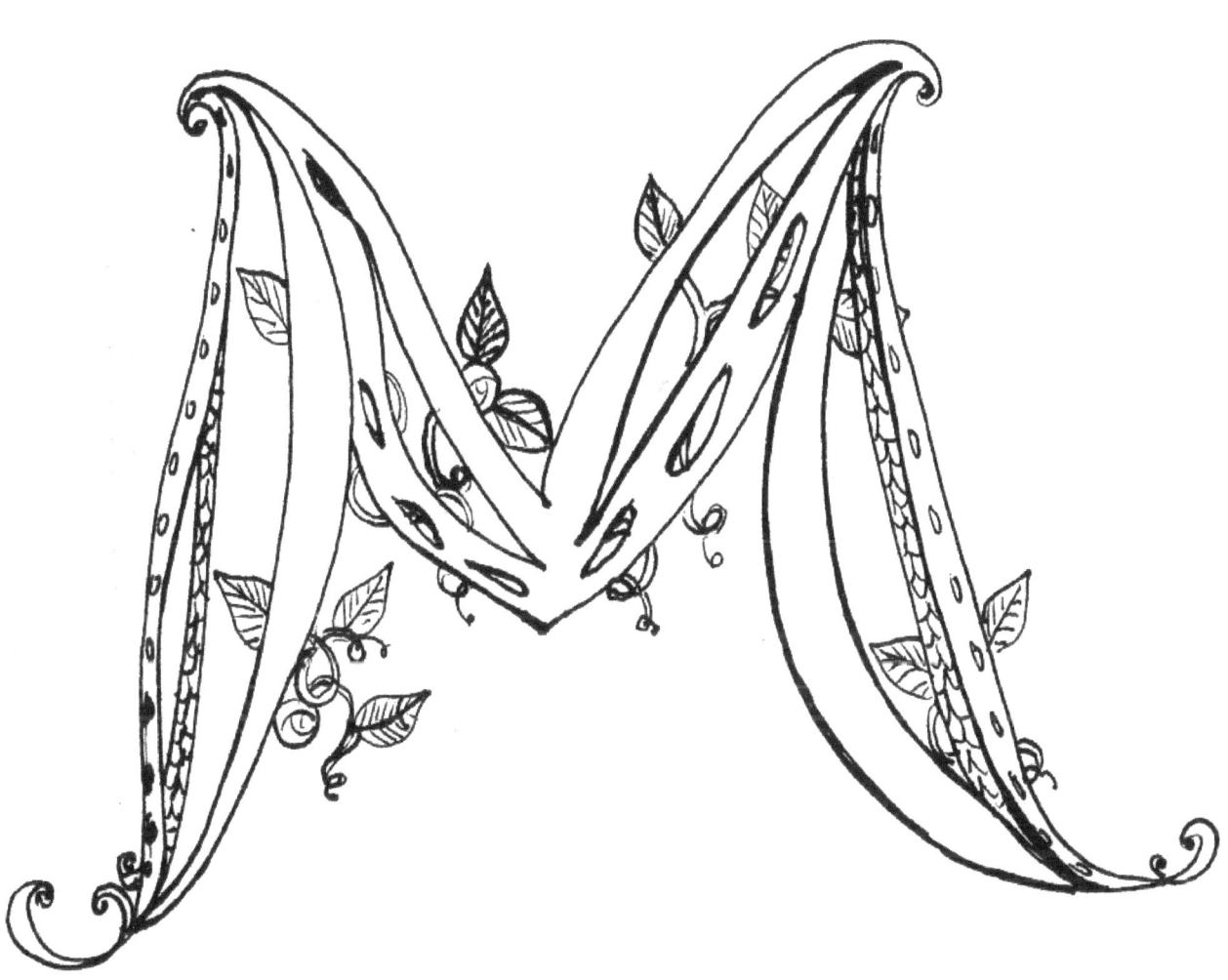

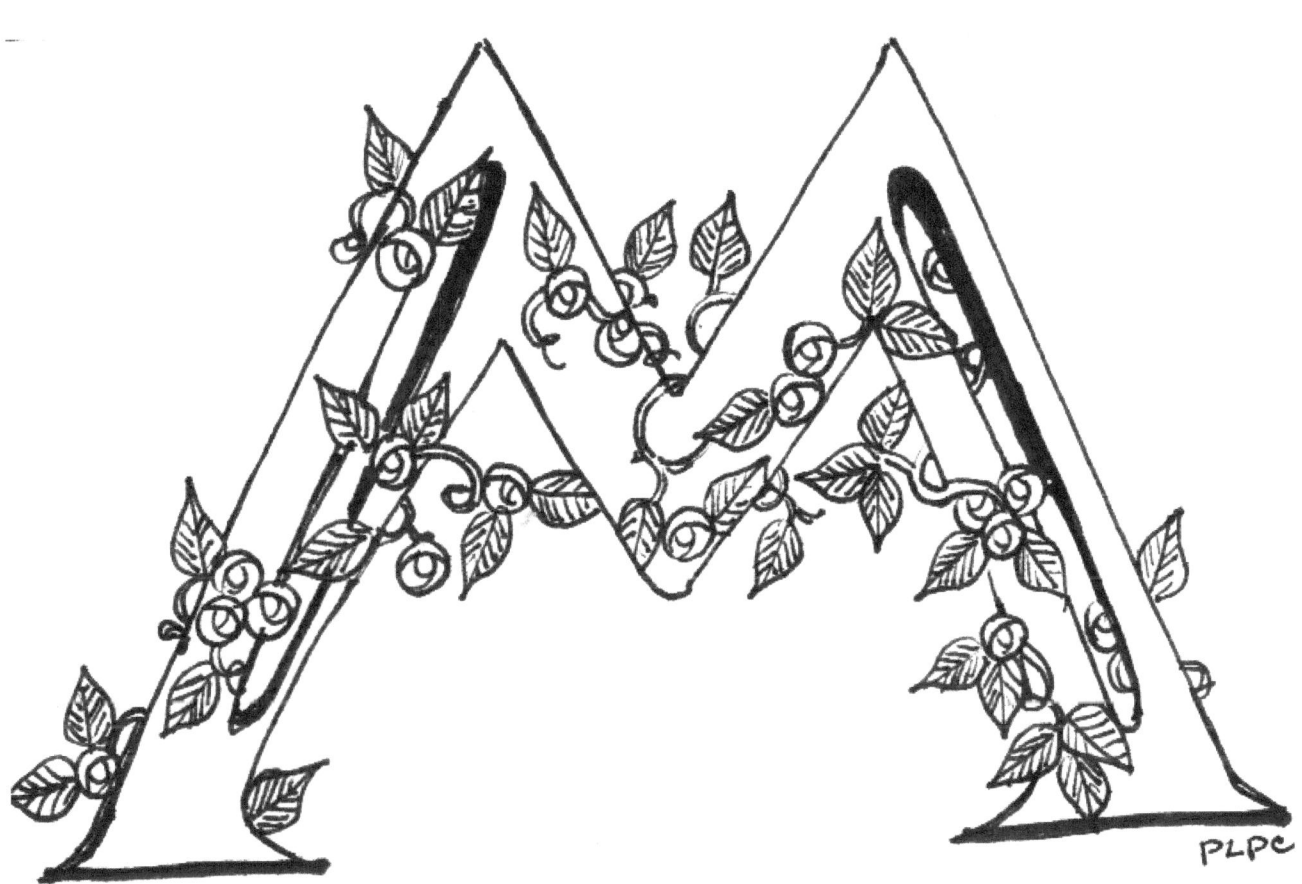

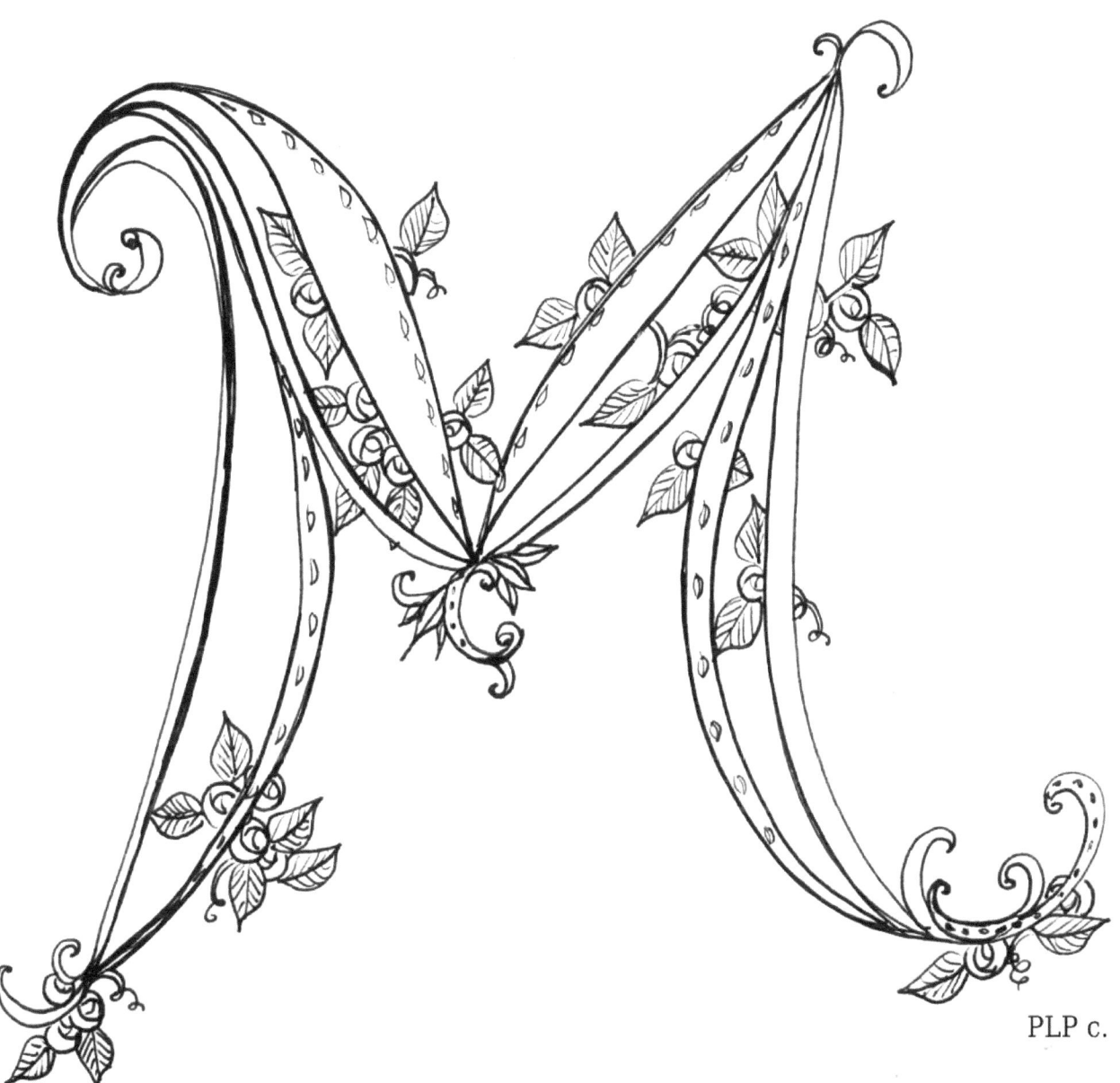

PLP c.

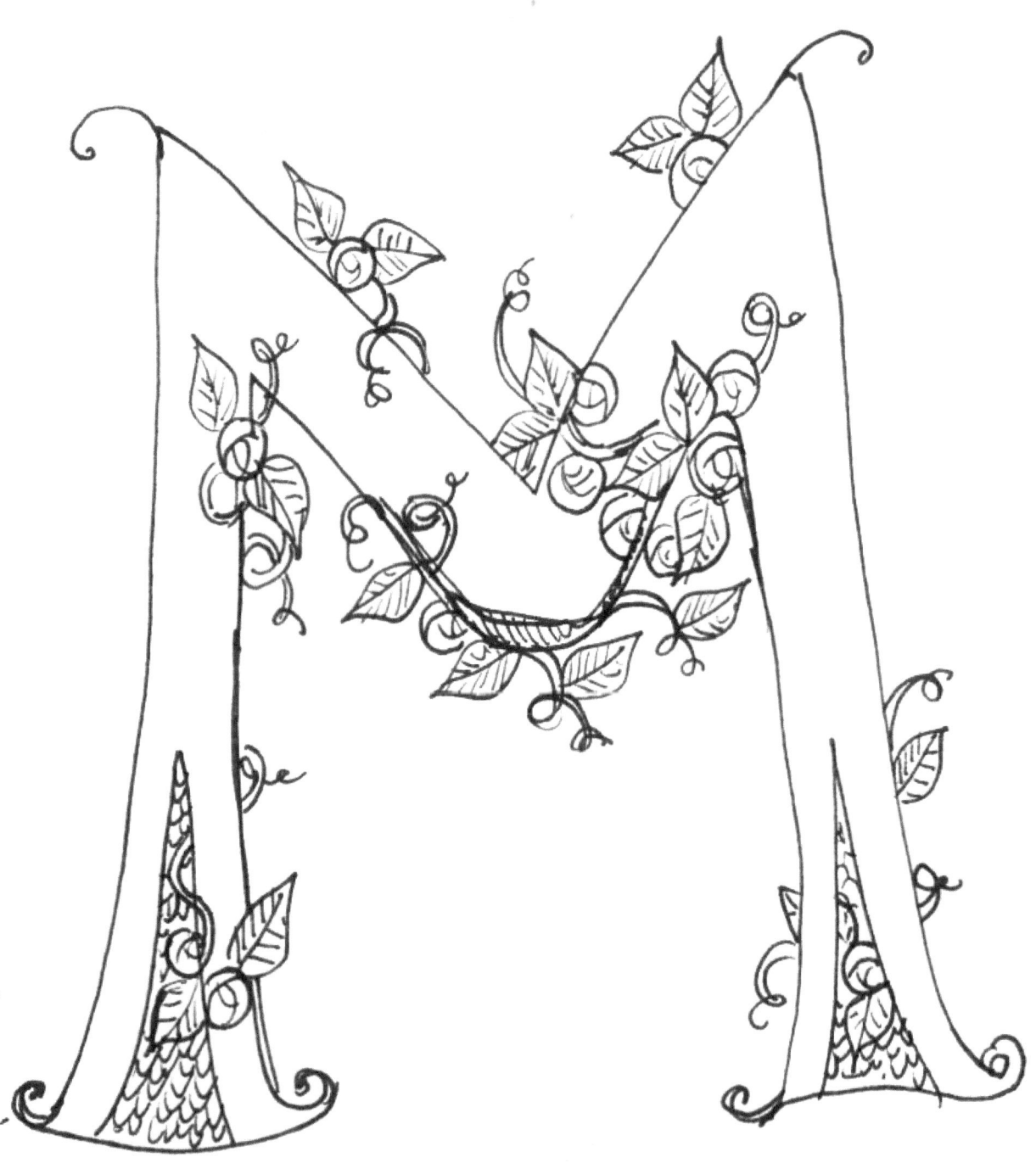

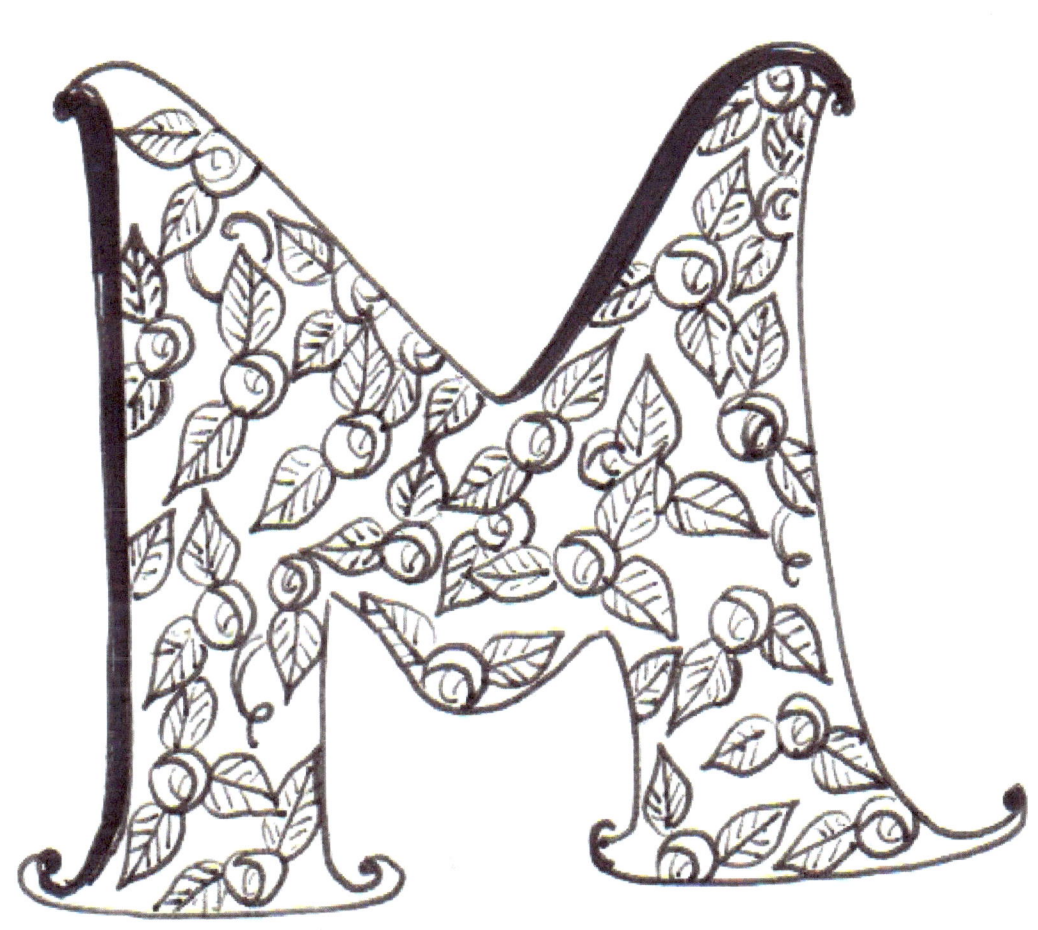

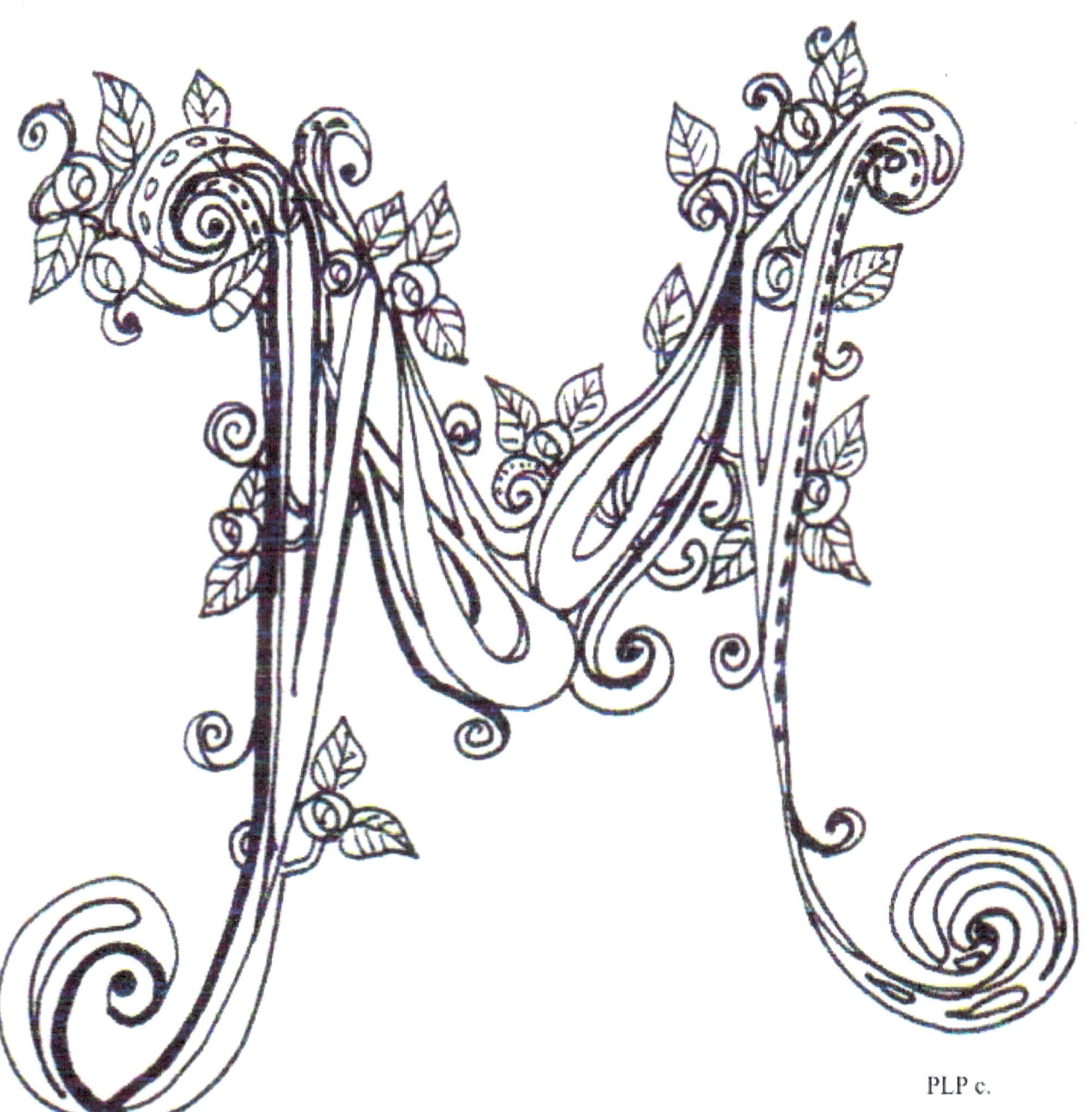

PLP c.

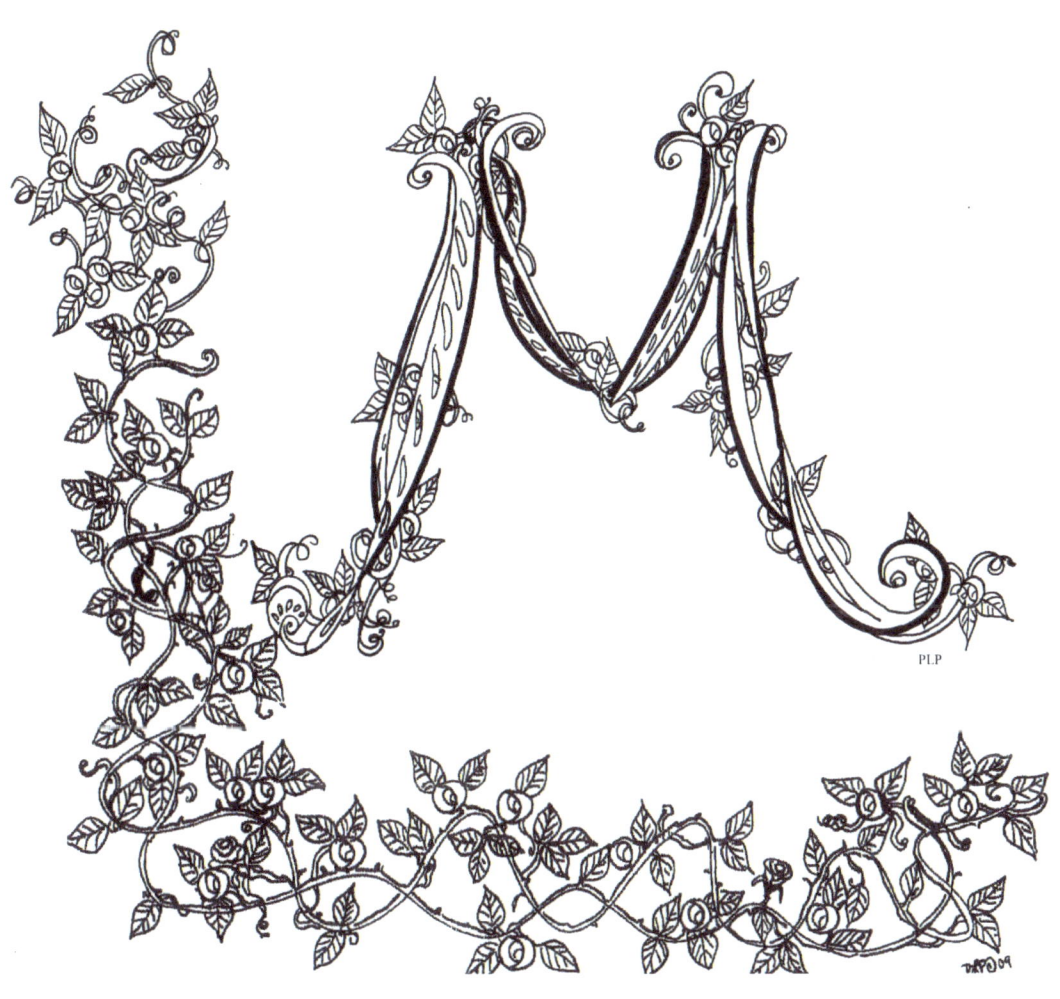

PLP

49

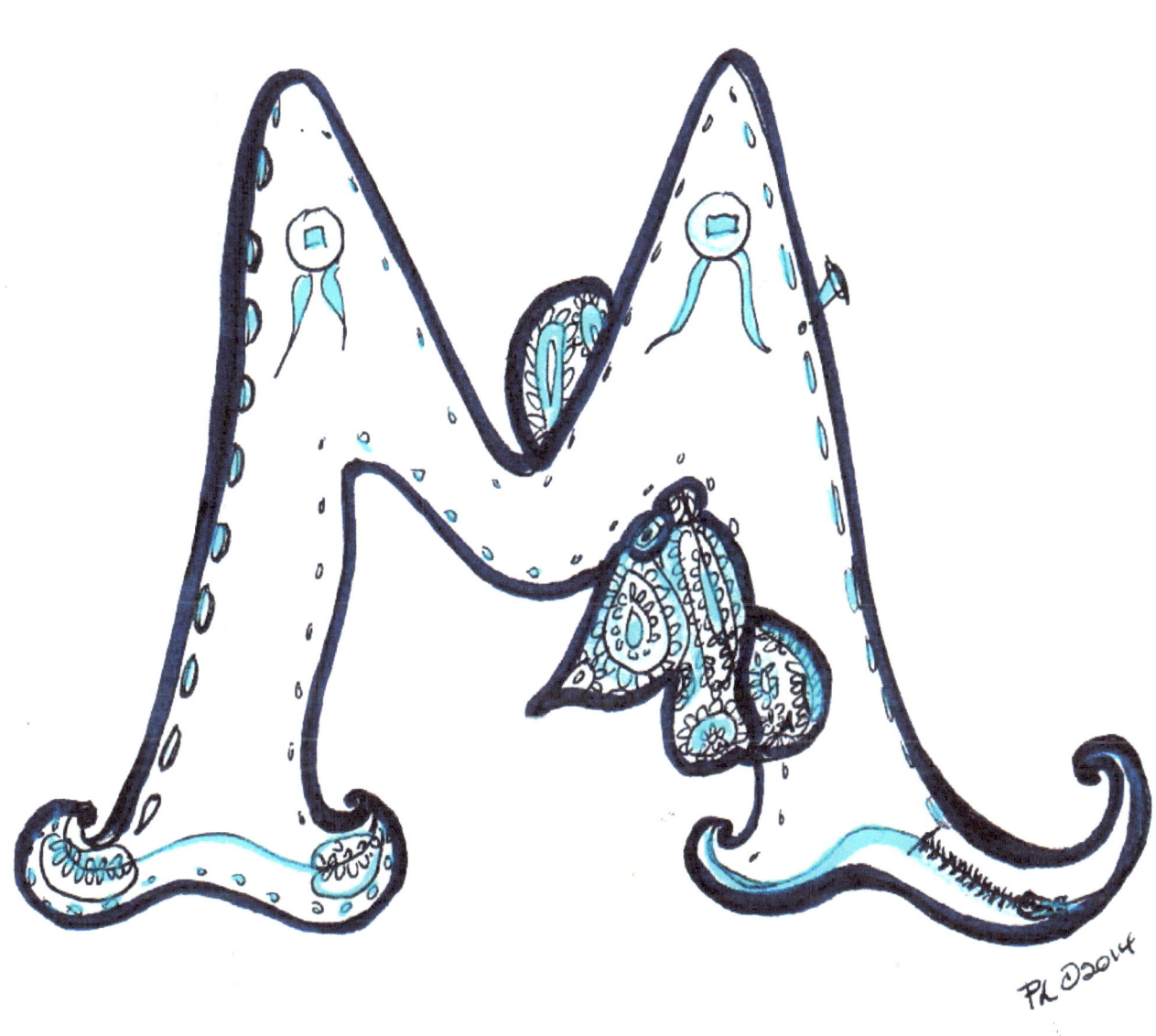

Have some fun with letter M.

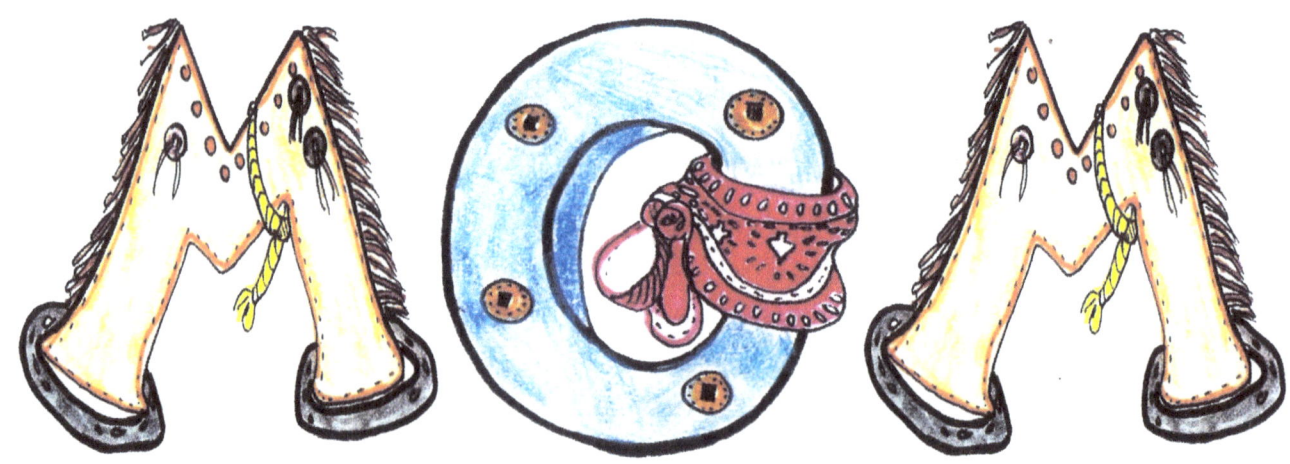

May this book of Letter M lead you into more and more

M possibilities!

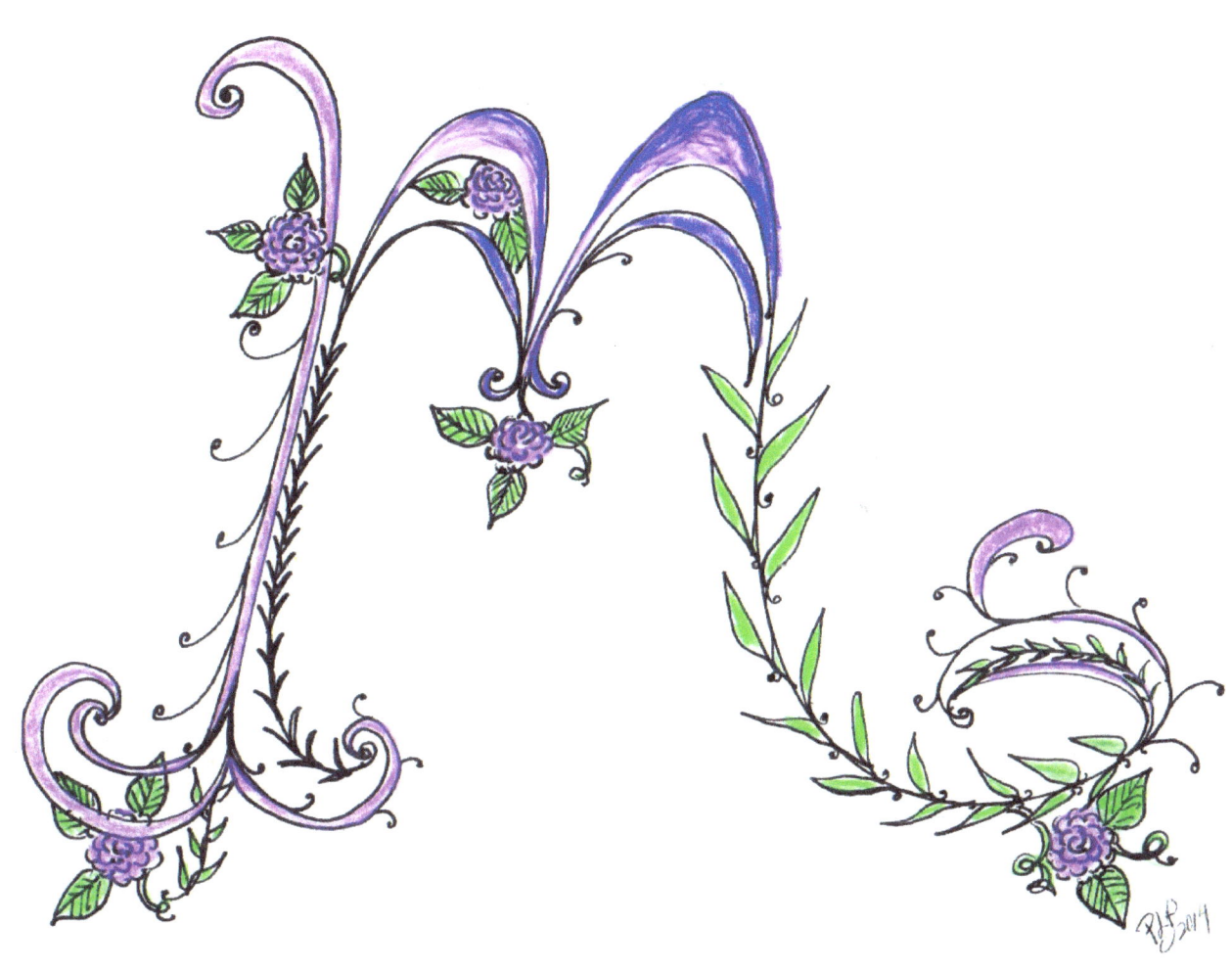

If you enjoyed The Majestic Letter M Book look for the other Letter Books by artist Peggy Louise Parrish.

Have more fun now than ever making M letters of your own...to color and enjoy.